Tech World

CELL PHONE
Pros and Cons

Lesley Ward

Publishing Credits

Rachelle Cracchiolo, M.S.Ed., *Publisher*
Conni Medina, M.A.Ed., *Managing Editor*
Nika Fabienke, Ed.D., *Series Developer*
June Kikuchi, *Content Director*
John Leach, *Assistant Editor*
Lee Aucoin, *Senior Graphic Designer*

TIME For Kids and the TIME For Kids logo are registered trademarks of
TIME Inc. Used under license.

Image Credits: p.8 Simon Rawles/Getty Images; all other images from
iStock and/or Shutterstock

Teacher Created Materials
5301 Oceanus Drive
Huntington Beach, CA 92649-1030
http://www.tcmpub.com
ISBN 978-1-4258-4977-1
© 2018 Teacher Created Materials, Inc.
Printed in China
Nordica.082019.CA21901097

Table of Contents

Connect to the World

People use their cell phones for many different reasons. They talk, send texts, take pictures, listen to music, and play games on their phones. They even use their cell phones to shop. The next time you are in a crowd, look around. Would you be surprised to see that most people are holding cell phones?

In some countries, many people do not have computers. They use their cell phones to browse the Internet. Phones that have these **capabilities** are called *smartphones*.

In the past, cell phones were very expensive, so only adults had them. But today many kids have their own phones. Owning a phone is a big responsibility—for kids and adults!

Get Mobile

The term *cell phone* comes from the way a phone works. Every phone links to a tower that is in the middle of an area called a *cell*. In some places, a cell phone is called a mobile phone.

I Need My Phone!

Some people worry a lot about being without their cell phones. Now there is even a special word to describe this feeling: *nomophobia*! This is a short version of "no mobile phone **phobia**."

Message

The Computer in Your Hand

A cell phone is a miniature computer. That means all the **components** inside the phone are miniature in size, too. Tiny microphones, microchips, and antennas fit inside the phone. Little transmitters and receivers send and receive signals.

Most people are not interested in how their cell phones work. They only care that their phones work when they need them. And people rely on their cell phones all the time. They use their phones as alarm clocks to wake them up. They look up stuff on the Internet, pay bills, and play games on their phones. Cell phones are truly amazing!

Watch That Phone

A smartwatch connects to your cell phone and to the Internet. It acts like a remote control. When you select apps on your smartwatch, it sends messages to your cell phone.

The First Cell Phone

The first cell phone was big. It weighed just under two pounds and was 13 inches tall. It was too heavy to carry around for very long. It was also expensive—it cost almost $4,000! Not many people could afford one.

Cell phones are built using many tiny parts.

Cell Phones Around the World

There are some places where people do not have access to computers. They use cell phones instead. They send messages to friends. They catch up on news and check the weather. Cell phones connect people to the rest of the world.

In Mexico, doctors use cell phones to send messages to patients and remind them to take their medicine. In Pakistan, farmers receive texts that tell them when to plant vegetables. In many African countries, people who don't have access to banks use their phones to track their money. Cell phones can help kids and adults around the world have better lives.

Caring for Cows

In Kenya, many farmers use their cell phones to keep their **livestock** healthy. Some use an app called iCow. It gives farmers advice about caring for their cows, chickens, sheep, and goats.

Message

OK

Flashlight in a Phone

In some places, many streets are poorly lit or without power. It can be scary to walk around after dark. The flashlight feature on most cell phones can light the way!

Safety Issues

Most kids use their cell phones to stay in touch with friends. They rarely think about their phones in terms of safety. But one of the main reasons parents let their kids have phones is safety.

In case of an emergency, you can call to get help right away. If you get lost or hurt, you can use your cell phone to call someone in your family. If you see an accident, you can contact the police.

This is all common sense, but sometimes people freeze during an emergency. **Panic** is a natural reaction. But it's important to remain calm and call for help. That's what cell phones are for!

ICE

It's a good idea to put an ICE (In Case of Emergency) contact in your phone. A person who helps you in an emergency will know to call this number right away. For example, you could store parents' numbers as "ICE Mom" and "ICE Dad."

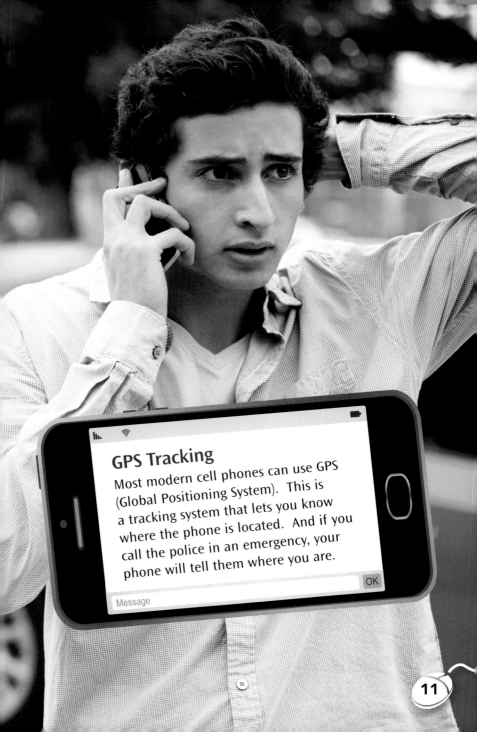

GPS Tracking

Most modern cell phones can use GPS (Global Positioning System). This is a tracking system that lets you know where the phone is located. And if you call the police in an emergency, your phone will tell them where you are.

OK

Message

Put Down the Phone

Some people spend too much time on their phones. They talk, text, and play games all day long with few breaks. When they feel bored, lonely, or worried, they pick up their phones. They're on their phones while watching television or doing homework. They even check their phones while driving, which is dangerous and against the law! These people have cell phone **addiction**.

Spending too much time on your cell phone is bad for your body and mind. Looking down at your phone screen for long periods of time can make your eyes tired and can hurt your back and neck. Using a phone before bedtime can make it hard to fall asleep. And not sleeping enough makes you tired and grouchy. Scientists discovered that cell phones give off small amounts of electrical waves called *radiation*. What does all this mean? People should limit their cell phone use.

Phones on Fire

A cell phone company made headlines in 2016. Some of its phones burst into flames. The phones had **defective** batteries that exploded when they became too hot. The company **recalled** millions of phones to keep phone users safe.

Message

OK

Loaded with Germs

Cell phones often have more germs and bacteria on them than toilet seats. Yuck! Germs can make you sick. Everyone should **disinfect** their cell phones regularly. Washing your hands before handling your phone is a good idea, too.

Fun with Cell Phones

Everywhere you go, people use their cell phones. They talk on their phones while walking down the street. They watch videos while sitting on a train. They check their email and texts while eating in a restaurant. It's strange to think that so many people do these things in public.

People also use the cameras on their phones. They take photos and videos of themselves and their friends. Sometimes, they post a funny photo or video on the Internet, and millions of people watch it. This is called *going viral*.

What if someone posted a photo or a video of you online? What if you were doing something embarrassing? Would you like it? Probably not!

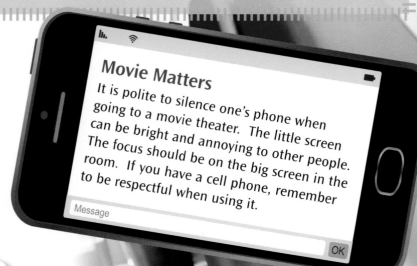

Movie Matters

It is polite to silence one's phone when going to a movie theater. The little screen can be bright and annoying to other people. The focus should be on the big screen in the room. If you have a cell phone, remember to be respectful when using it.

Message

OK

STOP! THINK...

> Can you think of places where using a cell phone is a bad idea?

> Should you be allowed to use a cell phone at school? Why or why not?

> No one likes it when people talk loudly on their phones in public. When you have to make a call in public, how can you show respect to those around you?

Personalized Cell Phones

Most people use their cell phones to show off their style. They choose a cool-looking phone case or cover. Luckily, cases and covers come in a lot of different colors and designs. Cell phones are **fragile**, so cases not only make phones look good, but they also offer protection.

Another way people personalize their phones is with the wallpaper, or the background on the main screen. Most people do not use the selection of patterns and photos that comes with the phone. Instead, they use a photo with people, animals, or sports logos. The best thing is that wallpapers can be changed anytime.

People can also select different ringtones for their cellphones. You may hear phones ring, buzz, or quack. Some phones sound like bells or crashing ocean waves. Popular songs can even be **downloaded** as ringtones.

quack, quack

buzz, buzz

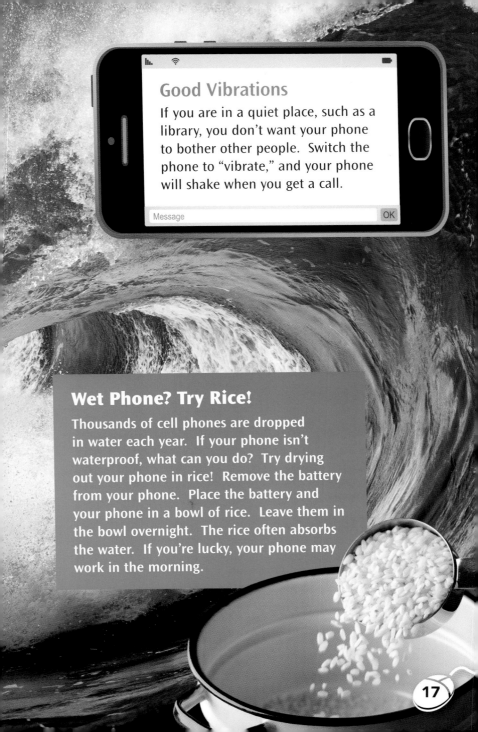

Good Vibrations

If you are in a quiet place, such as a library, you don't want your phone to bother other people. Switch the phone to "vibrate," and your phone will shake when you get a call.

Message | OK

Wet Phone? Try Rice!

Thousands of cell phones are dropped in water each year. If your phone isn't waterproof, what can you do? Try drying out your phone in rice! Remove the battery from your phone. Place the battery and your phone in a bowl of rice. Leave them in the bowl overnight. The rice often absorbs the water. If you're lucky, your phone may work in the morning.

ALL ABOUT THE APPS

App is short for *application*. It is a software program for your phone. You open apps by simply touching their **icons** on your phone screen. There are thousands of apps. Apps can be games, magazines, or newspapers. They can help you keep track of what you eat or stay in contact with friends. Many apps are free. Check out some types of apps that you can download on your phone.

 Educational apps teach subjects such as math or science.

 Television and movie apps let you watch your favorite shows on your phone.

 Map apps tell you where you are and give you directions.

 Game apps let you test your skills and battle your friends!

Weather apps tell you the forecast and the current outside temperature.

Social media apps connect you to your friends and family.

Music apps let you listen to your favorite tunes any time you want.

19

Kids and Cell Phones

Adults have different **opinions** on when their child should have a cell phone. All kids are different, so there is no perfect age to get a phone. It depends on how responsible you are.

Do you regularly break stuff or lose things like your homework? Do you have a hard time remembering where you put your belongings? If this sounds like you, don't be surprised if your parents say that you are not ready for a cell phone.

Your parents will likely make rules about your cell phone use. It's important to follow these rules because it shows that you can handle the responsibility of having a phone. One rule might be that you can use your cell phone only for a short amount of time each day.

Cell Phone Contract

You can show that you are responsible. Create a cell phone contract. Make a list of rules for phone use, and sign it. This will show that you are serious about owning a phone.

THINK LINK

Having your own cell phone is a **privilege**. Not every kid has a cell phone. If you have one, you must take care of it.

> How can a kid prove that he or she is ready to have a phone?
> What kind of rules might come with a cell phone?
> Do you think you are ready to have a phone? Why, or why not?

Cell phones come with some handy features. For example, most smartphone screens automatically lock. This stops people from using your phone without your permission. Your phone won't open until you tap in a special passcode. Only you and your parents should know your passcode.

If you are unable to answer your phone, an incoming call will go to your voicemail box. Record a voicemail greeting so the caller can leave a message. Most people say something such as, "Sorry I missed your call. I will call you back." You can be creative with your voicemail greeting, but make sure your parents approve of the one you make.

If it's all right with your parents, download some fun apps for your phone. Ask your friends about their favorite apps.

Where's My Phone?

Cell phones come with apps that help you find your phone if you lose it. You can simply sign in to a website that will locate your missing phone. It will show you the phone's location on a map.

Be Smart on Your Phone

It's a good idea to follow a few simple rules when you have a cell phone. These rules will keep you out of trouble.

✗ I will not give out information about myself on the phone.

✗ I will not respond to messages that are mean or make me feel nervous.

✗ I will not post photos or videos of other people without asking them first.

✗ I will not share my passwords with anyone except my parents.

✔ I will use my phone only when I am allowed.

✔ If I see someone use his or her phone dangerously, I will tell an adult.

✔ I will ask my parents before I download a new app.

✔ I will keep my phone in a safe place like my backpack or my pocket.

Stay Connected

Talk to your parents or grandparents about their lives before cell phones existed. Chances are that they will tell you that cell phones have made their lives a lot easier. Before, people needed to use paper maps to get to new places. These maps were hard to read. Now, a cell phone can give them exact directions! Grown-ups can quickly bank or shop on their phones, too. Gone are the days of waiting in line.

Don't forget that the tiny computer in your hand is a telephone! Use it to talk to people. It is important to stay in touch with your family and friends. Cell phones can be your connection to the world!

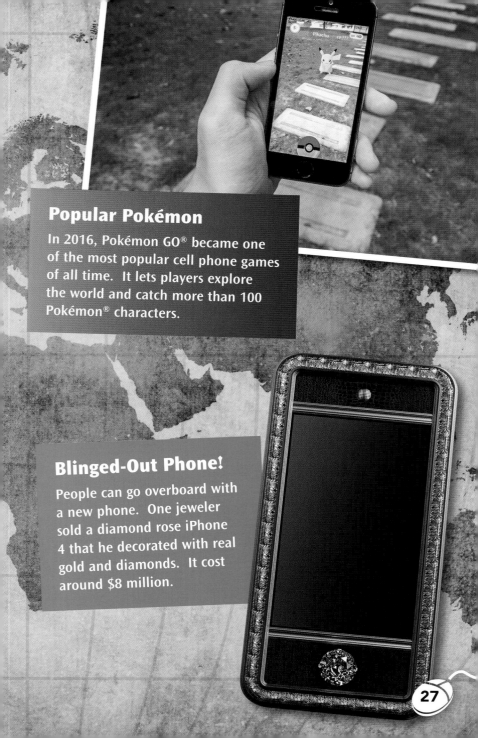

Popular Pokémon

In 2016, Pokémon GO® became one of the most popular cell phone games of all time. It lets players explore the world and catch more than 100 Pokémon® characters.

Blinged-Out Phone!

People can go overboard with a new phone. One jeweler sold a diamond rose iPhone 4 that he decorated with real gold and diamonds. It cost around $8 million.

Glossary

addiction—an unhealthy behavior that is hard to stop

capabilities—things that something can do

components—parts of a system

defective—having flaws

disinfect—to clean something by killing germs

downloaded—copied a file from the Internet

fragile—easily broken

icons—small images on a device's screen with an app logo on them

livestock—farm animals

opinions—views or ideas about something

panic—sudden, strong fear

phobia—an extreme fear of something

privilege—a special right that not everyone has

recalled—asked people to return a product because of a problem

Index

Check It Out!

Books

Bright, Bonnie. 2013. *Cellphoneitus*. Create Space Independent Publishing Platform.

Cook, Julia. 2012. *Cell Phoney*. National Center for Youth Issues.

Enz, Tammy. 2013. *The Amazing Story of Cell Phone Technology*. Capstone Press.

Videos

Amaya's Story—Using Cell Phones Wisely. www.commonsensemedia.org/videos/amayas -story-using-cell-phones-wisely.

TED Talks. *How Mobile Phones Can Fight Poverty*. www.ted.com/talks/iqbal_quadir_says _mobiles_fight_poverty.

Websites

Safe Kids. *10 Rules for Safe Family Cell Phone Use*. www.safekids.com/rules-for-family-cell -phone-use/.

Today I Found Out. *15 Fascinating Cell Phone-Related Facts You Probably Didn't Know*. www.todayifoundout.com.

Try It!

In 2016, when Natalie Hampton was 16, she created Sit With Us, an app that helps students find others to sit with at lunch. Natalie had been bullied in school and didn't want others to suffer the way she had.

If you could create an app, what problem would you want to solve?

- What would you name your app?
- How would it work?
- Share your app idea with a few friends.
- Use their feedback to improve your idea.

About the Author

Lesley Ward is an author and a former children's magazine editor. Now, she lives in the heart of Kentucky. She shares her farm with a lot of horses, cats, and dogs. She uses her cell phone to send lots of texts to family and friends. She also uses her phone to take cute pictures of all of her animals.